HEAR THE CREATOR'S SONG

A Guide to the Study Theme
Native Peoples of North America
with additional resources

Remmelt and Kathleen Hummelen

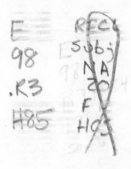

FRIENDSHIP PRESS • NEW YORK

ISBN 0-377-00151-1
Editorial Offices: 475 Riverside Drive, Room 772, New York, NY 10115
Distribution Offices: P.O. Box 37844, Cincinnati, OH 45237
Copyright © 1985 Friendship Press, Inc.
Printed in the United States of America

CONTENTS

**A Study Guide to the Theme
"Native Peoples of North America"**

Myths

Tradition

PREFACE

What are Native North Americans saying? How do they feel about the non-Native society surrounding them? What does it take to survive as Native people today?

Questions like these are discussed in the basic book for the study on Native Peoples of North America. We conducted the interviews that make up *Stories of Survival* realizing how much non-Native society needs to listen to Native people's voices, reflect and respond.

Hear the Creator's Song encourages such reflection and response. Six study sessions have been designed to enable leaders to use the basic book in small study groups. We assume that leaders will have limited time for their own planning; we also assume that there are skilled leaders within the group. If there is no person who feels she or he is able to plan the study sessions from this guide, a skilled leader from outside the group might be willing to help.

Hear the Creator's Song also includes a selection of poetry, artwork, myths, and articles from Native publications. These are not meant to provoke an anthropological exercise of identifying and comparing different traditions; rather, they point to the rich, diverse and intensely spiritual cultures out of which the men and women in *Stories of Survival* speak and occasionally reveal the pain of alienation from their heritage. These cultural reflections are an essential part of any study of the contemporary reality of Native North Americans.

The reader will note that throughout this study we have used the term "Native peoples" to refer to the original peoples of North America. Where the people interviewed in *Stories of Survival*—and the various organizations and concerns they represent—refer to "Native Americans", "Indigenous peoples", "Indians" etc. we have used these designations instead.

We would like to thank Brian Fraser of the Presbyterian Church in Canada for his help in preparing the biblical resources for this guide.

—Remmelt and Kathleen Hummelen

ABOUT THE BASIC BOOK

Stories of Survival is the main reference for the first four study sessions of this guide. It is a collection of profiles of Native men and women. Each profile includes some background on the speaker, occasionally a description of his or her childhood and early experiences relating to non-Native society. In most cases, one major issue is discussed from the perspective of the speaker's own experience. Other significant issues are raised as well. It is important to remember that Native people belong to some three hundred different nations, each having its own culture and history—so don't expect consistancy in the speakers' views or experiences. It is also important to note that each speaker's opinions are his or her's alone. They do not speak for anyone else, nor do they necessarily reflect these editors' points of view.

To help leaders identify where specific issues are addressed throughout the book, we have developed a Theme Index Chart (see page 16).

ABOUT THIS STUDY GUIDE

The six study sessions fall into two categories. Sessions one through four are designed as "core" sessions which should provide your group with a basis for sessions five and six. These last two have not been planned as formal sessions; their success will depend on your group's energies and interests.

Session One: Introduction to Native Peoples
Session Two: Spirituality
Session Three: Education
Session Four: Land/Economic Base
Session Five: Your Local Situation
Session Six: Native Peoples and Your Denomination

Each session is structured as follows:

A. *PRELIMINARY DISCUSSION:* During this time the preconceptions and values of non-Native society will be examined in relation to the topic. All participants should be able to join in this discussion since it is based on their own experiences and observations. We estimate that this discussion will take approximately ten minutes.

B. *LOOKING AT THE RESOURCE MATERIAL: Stories of Survival* is the primary resource, however speakers or audiovisuals could be arranged to provide supplementary background at this time. This section should take about thirty minutes.

C. *REFLECTION AND RESPONSE:* Twenty to thirty minutes.

Optional ideas are also suggested for groups having more time to prepare and carry out their programs.

Biblical reflections relating to the specific themes are suggested at the end of each of the first four sessions. These could be used as the focus of worship or meditation or introduced as part of the material to be discussed by the group.

AS YOU PLAN . . .

1. *Stories of Survival* is all you need, but the additional resources listed in the back of this guide will provide you with invaluable background and ideas for follow-up.

2. Identify your local resources. *The Native American Handbook* (see Bibliography) is particularly helpful in identifying reserves and reservations, regional organizations or Native centers in your area.

3. Check local libraries for publications and audio-visual resources. If what you find is not satisfactory, check the Bibliography. Some of the films we have listed may be expensive to rent, so plan to view them with the entire congregation or with neighboring churches or study groups.

4. Suggest that your group subscribe to *Akwesasne Notes, Washington Newsletter* and a local Native publication. *Akwesasne Notes* will provide a national and international overview, *Washington Newsletter* will keep you on top of current issues and legislation, and the local publication will help you begin session five. Start clipping articles on Native peoples from magazines and newspapers. Have a member of the group take responsibility for reading them and reporting back.

5. Start planning for sessions five and six at the beginning of the program year. Some of the group participants may volunteer to gather resources and make contacts early.

SESSION ONE: INTRODUCTION TO NATIVE PEOPLES

What you will need:
Large sheets of newsprint; selected excerpts from *Stories of Survival,* with enough copies to hand out to participants.

A. *PRELIMINARY DISCUSSION*
Non-Native society's perceptions of Native peoples.

Ask participants to brainstorm: What are some of the stereotypes, assumptions and preconceptions which non-Native people—both as individuals and as a society—have concerning Native peoples of North America? Respond with single words or short phrases. As the answers are given, list them on the left-hand side of the newsprint.

Go back over the list of responses and have participants identify where and how these ideas were formed (e.g. movies, history books, personal experiences). Write these down on the right-hand side of the newsprint.

If the participants do not respond readily, ask them questions like these: What images have we been given of Native peoples in history books? In movies? On T.V.? In advertising? What images come to our minds when we think of Native peoples' spiritual life? Social life? Economic life? Cultural life?

B. *USING OUR RESOURCES*
Excerpts from Stories of Survival; *How do Native people perceive non-Native society?*

Refer to the Theme Index Chart under the category "Non-Native Society" to identify those speakers whose stories would be best for the group to read at this time. If each participant does not have a copy of *Stories of Survival,* photocopy or type out enough quotations from the book so that each participant has a different speaker or quotation to refer to. You may want to use more than one excerpt from an individual's story. The excerpts should be long enough that participants will be able to understand the context of the quotation as well.

Give participants time to read their excerpts privately or aloud, depending on the group situation.

Ask participants to identify the ideas Native peoples have about non-Native peoples. Encourage them to respond with single words or brief phrases. List these ideas on the left-hand side of another sheet of newsprint.

Go back over the list and identify where and how these ideas were formed (e.g. movies, books, personal experiences).

C. REFLECTION AND RESPONSE

Take time to look at the two sheets of newsprint, the two sets of information. If the group is large, you may wish to break into small groups of three to five persons at this point. Allow time for reporting back if you do this. Ask the group:

- What do you notice about these perceptions?
- How do you feel as you read them?
- How do these attitudes affect who we are as individuals? As a community?
- What do these lists tell us about Native people? About ourselves?
- Is there anything we can do as individuals or as a group to dislodge negative perceptions and stereotypes?

PROGRAM OPTIONS

1. Along with *Stories of Survival* you may wish to use a film or other audiovisual as a resource for this session. (See resources listed at the end of this guide.) If you do this, choose a film that gives an overview of the issues concerning Native peoples today. In the *Reflection and Response* section, minor adjustments to the questions can be made to reflect these additional resources.

2. If you have plenty of time and an active group, divide participants into teams of two or three to visit a library, grocery store, bookstore or newstand to see what kind of treatment Native peoples receive in children's books, advertisements, greeting cards and product labels. One team should interview people in the library, stores or "on the street" to find out what *their* images are, and how these were formed. Have one team remain behind and prepare the *Using our Resources* section. When everyone returns, draw up the two lists as outlined and continue with *Reflection and Response*.

NATIVE PEOPLES IN A BIBLICAL CONTEXT

God called the church to be a blessing to all nations. "All" includes the three hundred nations of Native peoples in North America. In Jesus Christ, God showed us how that blessing was to be offered—by our being *with* people in relationships that enhance the God-given human dignity of each and every person.

How do the images of Native people you have identified in this section affirm the dignity of the Native people? How do these images deny it?

One of Jesus' greatest passions was for human dignity. He taught his followers to respect themselves as children of God and to treat all other human beings with the same respect. Psalm 8 is a confession of the God-given dignity of human beings. Read the psalm aloud:

O SOVEREIGN ONE, our God,
how majestic is your name in all the earth.

You whose glory above the heavens is chanted
 by the mouths of babes and infants,
you have founded a bulwark because of your foes,
 to still the enemy and the avenger.

When I look at your heavens, the work of your fingers,
 the moon and the stars which you have established;
what are human beings that you are mindful of them,
 and mortals that you care for them?

Yet you have made them little less than God,
 and crowned them with glory and honor.
You have given them dominion over the works of your hands;
 you have put all things under their feet,
 all sheep and oxen,
 and also the beasts of the field,
the birds of the air, and the fish of the sea,
whatever passes along the paths of the sea.

O SOVEREIGN ONE, our God,
 how majestic is your name in all the earth.

Pray the psalm silently as a confession of your worth as a human being.

Pray the psalm silently again as a confession of the worth of all human beings.

Pray the psalm aloud *together* as a confession of one another's worth.

Pray the psalm once more in silence, this time mindful that the dominion given to us as human beings is a trust from God and is to be used as a blessing to all nations.

SESSION TWO: SPIRITUALITY

What you will need:
Copies of specified profiles to hand out to each member of the group; newsprint.

A. *PRELIMINARY DISCUSSION*
The influence of religion on the values and relationships of non-Native society.

Ask participants to discuss how their religious beliefs shape their relationships with other individuals, with the community, with the environment, with their possessions, with their cultural life.

B. *USING OUR RESOURCES*
Spiritual values of Native peoples are expressed by most of the speakers in Stories of Survival.

Divide participants into three groups. Have enough copies of the basic book or copies of the profiles of Douglas Long and Art Solomon, and either Jim White, Harrel Davis or Stan McKay so that each group can focus on one of these individuals. Allow them time to read the profiles. Then ask them to discuss the following questions in each group:
   • What are some of the main concepts in traditional Native spirituality?
   • What are some problems experienced by Native people when they practice their beliefs?
   • Does the person whose profile you read see a conflict between Native spiritual ways and Christianity? Between Native spiritual ways and the larger society? What are these conflicts? How do they feel about them?
   • How does the person whose profile you read resolve the conflict?
   Bring the groups back together and have each report back along with a brief background of the person for the benefit of the other groups. Write responses on newsprint for reference in the next section.

C. *REFLECTION AND RESPONSE*

Remain in the larger group or break into small groups and discuss the following questions. If using small groups, allow time for reporting back and considering the last question together.

- How do we feel as we hear these experiences? Why?
- What would we say to each of these speakers from our own non-Native experience?
- What can we learn from these individuals?
- What can we do about the issues they raise?

PROGRAM OPTION

If there is time, the myths and legends that follow could be introduced in the *Using our Resources* section as the first source from which to identify spiritual values. Then the groups could look into the profiles. The myths and legends should be read aloud—in particular, "When the World was Small." Compare this to the Old Testament story of Creation, which is part of the biblical reference for this session. See the resources listed in the back of this book for books, records and tapes of other myths and legends.

NATIVE SPIRITUALITY IN A BIBLICAL CONTEXT

God created the heavens and the earth and declared it was good. This is the first and foremost affirmation in the Bible about the world in which we live. It was reaffirmed in the covenant with Noah following the near-destruction of Creation. And it is the ground, literally and figuratively, out of which Christian spirituality should grow.

Psalm 104 is a hymn of praise to the Creator God. It is an hymn of praise to the interdependence of the earth that was God's pleasure to create.

Read the psalm silently and create a mental picture of the network of nature it describes as it sustains life on the planet.

Read the psalm verse by verse, each person in the group reading one verse. Listen for the everyday earthiness of this hymn of praise.

Pray the psalm silently as your own acknowledgement of the goodness of the creation.

Pray the Psalm verse by verse, as before, as a commitment to the preservation of what God has declared good. Pay special attention to the final condemnation of those whose actions deny this affirmation.

SESSION THREE: EDUCATION

What you will need:
Copies of specified profiles to hand out to each member of the group

A. *PRELIMINARY DISCUSSION*
Education and non-Native people.

Have participants discuss the following questions:
- What is the purpose of education?
- Whose values should our educational system teach? What are some of these values?
- Who should participate in making decisions about what is taught in our schools?

B. *USING OUR RESOURCES*
Education is the main focus of several of the speakers in Stories of Survival.

Divide participants into four groups. Have each group work on one of the following profiles: Paulette Fairbanks, Yvonne Beamer, LaDonna Harris and Kirk Kickingbird. Make sure each person has a copy of the profile he or she is working on.
Fairbanks and Beamer both speak about the public school system. Have those two groups consider these questions:
- What are the key issues your speaker raises about the educational system and its effects on young Native people?
- What suggestions does she make for change?
Harris and Kickingbird are involved with community and adult education. Have these two groups discuss these questions:
- What are the key educational and social issues for the communities that your speaker works with? Name some of the conflicts in values that these communities are experiencing.
- How are these communities meeting the challenge?
- What blocks or hindrances are they experiencing?
Have each of the four groups report back, starting with those working with Fairbanks and Beamer.

C. *REFLECTION AND RESPONSE*

In the following discussion make sure both Native and non-Native education are considered.
- What is your gut reaction to the situations these speakers have described?
- What do these stories tell us about the way we have built up non-Native society?

• What are they telling us about ourselves?

• Refer to the suggestions Fairbanks and Beamer make. Are there ways in which your group can implement some of these?

PROGRAM OPTIONS

1. If the myths and legends at the back of this book are not used in session two, they can be read aloud at this point. Discuss the educational function they would have in communicating values. Identify the specific values these legends pass on. The biblical reference suggested for this session provides an interesting parallel to the role of Native legends. This option may be used as the opening exercise for *Using our Resources*—then proceed as outlined.

2. If your group enjoys role-playing and you have time to do some preliminary preparation, the following suggestion could work well in the *Using our Resources* section.

Setting: A meeting of the local school board. On the agenda is a concern brought by a group of parents from a local Native community. They speak about the problems their children are having in the local school. Participants in the role-play include:

• Two representatives of the parents' group who bring with them a written complaint and a proposal for changes. (Use the situations Fairbanks and Beamer recall to get background on what such a concern might be.)

• Chairperson of the school board who should be prepared to "chair" the meeting.

• Members of the board (four or five, depending on the size of your group) They should be prepared to raise all the problems in responding to the concern or complaint and proposal.

• The public. The rest of the group can participate by supporting one side or the other as they would in a real meeting. Some could represent business interests, some could be church members, teachers, etc.

See if you can reach a consensus on whatever action the board should take.

Afterwards, discuss how each participant felt in his or her role, how she or he reacted to the other actors.

Proceed with the questions raised above: the key issues raised and the suggestions made; then proceed with *Reflection and Response.*

NATIVE EDUCATION IN A BIBLICAL CONTEXT

God is a storyteller. That's what we have in the Bible: the people of God telling the stories of God. And when God came to us and lived with us in Jesus Christ, stories remained the focal point of the teachings. Take, for example, the story of the Good Samaritan (Luke 10:25-37) The last time I heard the story told, the characters had changed. The setting was the Wild West; the priest and Levite were a minister and an elder in the church and the Samaritan was a Native person. The heart of the story was still the fear and religious scruples that stood in the way of one human being treating another human being with dignity and compassion.

Take a few minutes and recast the story of the Good Samaritan in our present context, using characters you have come across in this study.

Tell the story to the others in the group, moving from person to person until everyone has told his or her version of the story.

Reflect in silence on what these stories of our communities mean for the life of our community.

Part with these words to each other: *Go in peace and let us be a blessing to our neighbors.*

SESSION FOUR: LAND/ECONOMIC BASE

A. *PRELIMINARY DISCUSSION*
Attitudes of non-Native peoples towards land

Refer to the biblical references for this session and discuss the following questions:

● What do these Old Testament passages say about land and how we use it?

● Does the biblical concept of Jubilee seem harsh to you?

● Are there any present-day parallels to the situation of land being used as a "trust" rather than "owned"?

● How do you personally think of, feel about and experience land?

B. *USING OUR RESOURCES*
Land and the practice of sovereignty over that land are major issues discussed throughout Stories of Survival.

Review the traditional spiritual view of land. The group should recall this as part of the discussion on Native spirituality in session two. Then begin to talk about the traditional use of land and how land became the economic base for the community (e.g. for agriculture, hunting, and trapping). To do this, refer to speakers listed in the Theme Index Chart under "Native Spirituality" and "Culture". A helpful addition would be a display map (see resource listing) outlining the various regions of the continent and showing how Native peoples' land base differed from place to place.

Divide the participants into three groups. Have group one refer to Sampson's profile; group two should be given the profile of one or more of those speakers listed under "Treaties" in the Theme Index Chart; group three should refer to the story of one or more of those speakers listed under "Natural Resources".

Group one: Discuss how Native people made the transition from a traditional economy to a capitalist economy. What have been the feelings and reactions of different groups of Native people at various points throughout this transition?

Group two: According to the people whose profiles you have before you, what were the reasons Native people entered into treaties? How did Native people view these treaties? Who signed them, on both sides? With what authority? How have treaties been broken? Why? (Make sure the point is raised that Native people wanted to protect their traditional way of life, therefore treaties included their rights to hunt, fish, trap, etc.)

Group three: What are the issues faced by Native people when natural resource development takes place on their reserves or reservations?

Have the groups report back in the order stated above so it becomes apparent how the traditional-to-capitalist pattern develops over a period of time.

C. *REFLECTION AND RESPONSE*

Consider the following questions:
- What would be the reasons given by government officials, politicians and business people for their actions in regard to Native land?
- Are any of these attitudes changing? How? Why or why not?
- What would your response be to a government or business representative in regard to their concept of land?
- Is there any action your group can take to respond to Native people's concern for their land base?

PROGRAM OPTION

See resource listings at the back of this book to order one of the many excellent films on the topic of traditional ways and the economic and cultural impact of mining or pipeline projects.

From the Exodus. . .

. . . I have come to deliver them out of the hand of the Egyptians, and to bring them up out of that land to a good and broad land, a land flowing with milk and honey . . . (Exodus 3:8)

. . . to the Exile . . .

. . . I will put my Spirit within you, and you shall live, and I will place you in your own land; then you shall know that I, the Lord, have spoken, and I have done it . . . (Ezekiel 37:14),

. . . a land in which people could live and prosper was central to the God's promises to Israel. The land had been created for a blessing and was to be used as a blessing. It was never "owned" in the sense we have developed the concept of owning land, but held as a trust from God. Hence, the law of Jubilee: Every seventh year, the land was given a rest, slaves were released and debts were forgiven. Every fiftieth year, even more happened:

> And you shall hallow the fiftieth year, and proclaim liberty throughout the land to all its inhabitants; it shall be a jubilee for you, when each of you shall return to his property and each of you shall return to his family. (Leviticus 25:1-17)

The intention of Jubilee year was that people should not harm or wrong each other. It was the law of the Lord.

By the time of the writing of the New Testament, wealth had replaced land as the focus for Jesus' ethical teachings. But the principles remained the same: What we have is the Lord's, to be used for God's glory as a blessing to all nations.

Reflect in silence.

SESSION FIVE: YOUR LOCAL SITUATION

For this session we encourage you to investigate a local or regional issue of concern to Native people and, if possible, to visit a reservation or reserve.

The visit should be planned well in advance. Contact the local band council (in Canada) or tribal office (in the United States) to make arrangements. Discuss with them some of the things you would like to see and talk about. It may be possible to visit the school or health service and talk with staff and students. If your group is large, it might be less disruptive to break into small teams with each focusing on a different area.

This visit, as well as the first four study sessions, should give you a starting point for discussing a local or regional issue. In case you have trouble pointing to such an issue, here are some questions to help your investigation.

1. How do the Native people you meet feel about the relationship between their reservation (or reserve) and the non-Native community near the reservation? What is their relationship with the state or province in which the reservation is located? With the federal government? Try to get a grasp of the *feelings* as well as the facts.

2. What opportunities are there on the reserve for both formal and non-formal education? Do children have to leave the reserve to continue their education? If so, at what age? Where do they have to go? How do they feel about this? Who makes decisions about education on the reserve? In what language is schooling conducted?

3. What about health and other social services? Who controls these? In what language are these services provided?

4. What is the economic base of the reserve? Are there any projects to develop natural resources? If so, what impact have they had on life on the reserve?

5. How much of the population of the reservation is able to find work? Where? What kind of work do people do?

6. What religious groups or denominations are present on the reservation? How long have they been there? How do Native people feel about the presence of these groups or denominations? What role do they play in the community? (Let the people you meet know you want a serious reply and not one to make you feel good!) Are traditional ceremonies still practiced? Ask the people on the reservation to tell you about some of these. Not all ceremonies are open to everyone, nor are details considered public information.

7. What is the nature of government on the reserve? If it is not traditional, why did it change? When? How? What are the responsibilities of the government? What responsibilities would the Native people *like* to have? What do they consider to be the key issues for their community?

8. Are there ways in which your group can support the concerns of the reservation you have visited?

If you live in an area where Native people do not live on a reservation, there are other questions you might ask to start a discussion: What is the situation between these Native people and the non-Native population surrounding them? Are there any special services provided to them? Do any Native people participate in the decision-making processes of the county or town in which they live?

If there are few Native people in your area, ask: Why did Native people leave this part of the country? Were they forced?

If there are no reservations, find out why not. Were there at one time? Were Native people "kicked off" their land? Why are there so few reservations east of the Mississippi?

If you live in a city, find out where Native people live. Find out why they are there, where they came from.

SESSION SIX: NATIVE PEOPLES AND YOUR DENOMINATION

This session is suggested as an opportunity to look at your denomination's involvement with Native peoples. Here are some comments for you to consider when you contact your church headquarters for information.

The past: Neither guilt-trips nor triumphalism are appropriate responses. We must recognize that while we can celebrate the individuals who shaped the histories of our nations and regions, we cannot ignore the impact that their activities had on the original nations of this continent.

The present: What are we involved in now? What kinds of concerns do your church's programs respond to? Do these reflect the issues your group has identified over the course of this study? Are Native people fully involved in your denomination's structure and decision-making processes?

The future: As we reflect on past experiences and grow more aware of present issues we can renew our commitment to engage in creative, innovative action. What do you think your congregation or denomination should be doing in its ministry with Native peoples? What can your study group do to help the denomination move in this direction?

THEME
INDEX
CHART

Themes:

1. CHRISTIANITY
2. CULTURE
3. EDUCATION
4. GOVERNMENT
5. HISTORY
6. LAW
7. NATIVE SPIRITUALITY
8. NATURAL RESOURCES
9. NON-NATIVE SOCIETY
10. RACISM
11. RESERVATIONS
12. SOVEREIGNTY
13. SUGGESTIONS
14. TREATIES
15. VALUE-CONFLICT
16. WOMEN

Author	1	2	3	4	5	6	7	8	9	10	11	12	13	14	15	16
ANGECONEB	✳								✳							
FAIRBANKS	✳	✳			✳				✳			✳				
SNIPP		✳	✳		✳				✳			✳				
DELORIA	✳	✳			✳				✳			✳	✳			
THEOBALD					✳				✳							
TWO-AXE EARLY	✳								✳							✳
SAMPSON	✳	✳					✳		✳		✳	✳				
LONG							✳		✳							
SOLOMON							✳		✳		✳	✳				✳
OXENDINE		✳							✳		✳	✳				
ANOEE	✳						✳		✳							
DUPRIS	✳						✳		✳		✳					
BEAMER	✳	✳							✳	✳	✳	✳				
LESTER						✳			✳			✳				
KICKINGBIRD	✳	✳			✳				✳		✳	✳	✳			
HARRIS					✳	✳			✳			✳			✳	✳
WHITE	✳	✳			✳				✳		✳	✳	✳			
DAVIS	✳	✳			✳		✳		✳							
MCKAY		✳					✳		✳		✳	✳	✳			
ROUGHFACE		✳							✳							
LAPOINTE		✳	✳						✳				✳			✳

16

Left, a bone-carver (photo by Semeonie Sivuarapik, Northern Affairs, Canada); Center, an artist at work; bottom, a child does traditional beadwork.

MYTHS

When the World was Small
And How It Grew
by Ernest Benedict

It is in the winter time that the best stories are told, when dark comes early and children stay where it is warm and all the family has gathered. The summer months are used to prepare for these times. Food and fuel and home repairs and clothing are made ready when days are long and the outdoors welcome the people. Then, when all has been done that needs to be done in the soft season, there is the certain change to a harder, sterner way of life. The fires need to be kept going, the warm clothing and blankets are put to use, and the family remembers far back and plans for the distant future.

And so it is at this time that a child will climb onto the lap of an elder and ask, "Grandpa, where did the world come from?"

There is an Iroquois answer to that question. It has been recorded in the memories of generations of elders. It is recorded in the designs of beaded decorations on clothing. It is a favorite theme of Iroquois artists.

Once there was a great land where there lived great and wonderful people. This land was up above the sky in a world that was always day.

The light that shone in the sky-world came from a great tree that had blossoms so bright that no other light was needed. There was peace and plenty and no death in that sky-world. However, there came a time when peace and comfort was disturbed by anger and jealousy.

The wife of the chief was soon to become a mother, but such a thing had not happened for such a long time that she did not know what was happening. She did not know what to tell the chief, her husband. After all, when people lived forever, they did not need to bring children into the sky-world. So Sky-woman, being confused, kept her secret.

Then the chief began to be suspicious about Sky-woman's secret. She was too nervous when near him. She spent so much time daydreaming. She did not answer his questions as freely. And so his suspicions grew. She must have been unfaithful! She must be punished.

Sky-woman sat by herself near the great tree of the bright blossoms. She was lost in her daydreams. Then the old chief grew very angry. He went and uprooted the tree. He just pulled it right up out of the ground of this sky-world. There was a great hole where the tree had been. The blossoms continued to shine into the hole. The light shone through the hole into the world below.

Sky-woman was startled out of her daydreams. She looked with curiosity down into the hole, saw the lower world down below her. She did not notice that her husband, the chief, was angry. And so in great surprise, she found herself pushed into the hole!

In the world below, there was water, a great ocean that stretched all across underneath the sky-dome. There was no land. There were water animals and fishes and water birds. These had lived until this time in a dark wet world. All these creatures were startled when the sky tree was uprooted and light came down all around them and they saw each other for the first time.

Then they were even more surprised when they saw Sky-woman falling down through the hole in the sky.

There was a hasty meeting held and the water birds acted with one mind. They flew up as high as they could and with the geese in the center, locked their wings together and caught Sky-woman and carried her slowly down toward the water below.

The water animals also were busy. They had decided to try to make some dry place for Sky-woman. But the only earth they knew about was at the bottom of the ocean!

The water animals, one by one dove down as far as they could go. The otter found nothing, the beaver tried but he came back exhausted. It was the little muskrat who dove down and came back up dead, but in his paw was found a little bit of earth from the bottom of the sea!

Quickly, the earth was put on the back of the great sea-turtle. Then, as he began to grow, the earth grew with him and at last there was a place where Sky-woman could rest and live out her days. And so it was that on this land on the back of the turtle, the human beings had their beginning.

Yes the Sky-woman had good things to eat. The land of the sky-world is a carpet of strawberries. The last move that Sky-woman was able to make as she began her fall to earth was to grasp some of the strawberry plants, bringing them with her. These grew well on earth and Sky-woman did not grow hungry for this was the food of the sky-world.

Today the strawberry is still honored in a special ceremony of thanksgiving. At this time, it has special power to heal the body and spirit of believers. It is still a common saying among those who remember a near relative who has passed on into the spirit world, "He or she has gone back to pick strawberries!" "So hiak on" or "Tsio-hiak-on!"

But the story does not end there. Sky-woman gave birth to twin boys. One was Toroniawagon, "Holder of the Heavens", the other, Sawiskara, "The Spoiler". While Toroniawagon went about creating all things of nature, the beautiful scenery, animals, birds and plant life, Sawiskara created only the angry, dangerous and ugly.

Thus, the wolverine is a very strong animal, very intelligent, but Sawiskara also gave him a nasty temper and an enormous appetite. The medicine plants grow in the midst of those that will make you sick. The beautiful lakes can contain dangerous currents of wind and water. A quiet shady grove of trees may contain a cloud of hungry mosquitos. These are the works of Sawiskara, he who could not create the useful, the life-giving, the beautiful, but only things that would detract from the best.

When human beings were created, Toroniawagon gave long life, a useful body, skills beyond any other creature, intelligence almost equal to his own. So many wonderful things were combined in this human being.

Sawiskara was not to be pushed aside however. He gave a great capacity to lie and cheat and to fight, greater than any other creature, and it seemed that again Sawiskara had spoiled this wonderful creature.

But Toroniawagon was able to repair his creation. He gave a freedom to choose. So today, the people of earth have come through their long history full of good things. They have increased in numbers. They have become rulers over all of creation. They have greater skills than ever before. They know more now than can be gathered in any one place. They also have been in constant trouble in every generation. They have fought so hard that they were in danger of killing every creature on earth. The more they learned, the more likely it was that the new knowledge would be used to fight and to inflict harm on each other.

Let us hope that the plans of the Holder of the Heavens will not be destroyed. Let us pray that all people will use their freedom to choose. Let us all choose to behave as the Holder of the Heavens has planned; to be the last and greatest work of the Creator!

Originally published in Tawow, *Vol. 7, No. 1,* Indian and Northern Affairs, *Canada. Reprinted with permission.*

Winter and Summer

retold by Lenore Keeshig-Tobias

Long, long ago, in ancient times, a giant came down from the northland to settle in Glooskap's country. This giant, who was older than he could remember, brought blizzards as he huffed and puffed his way south. Soon everything was covered in deep white and chilling snow and since the people had not experienced Winter before, they were quite unprepared for the climatic change. All activity stopped as Winter breathed deeply and his breath hung in the air. The people grew fearful of this old man as their wood supply and foliage for the animals became more and more deeply buried under snow. With food supplies dwindling and lodge fires giving little warmth, the people began to die.

Glooskap was greatly distressed for, as powerful as he was, he could do nothing to save his beloved people. Finally, as a last resort, he decided to go and persuade, or bribe if necessary the giant into returning to his own country. Clutching his moose robe about him tightly and setting out alone, Glooskap journeyed for many days and many nights in search of Winter's lodge.

When he finally found it, it was a sight to behold! Glooskap stepped inside. Yet in spite of his power and determination, he soon succumbed to the old man's frosty charms and fell in love with the crystal lodge.

Winter could weave such tales, tales of the olden times before people existed when the whole country was as sparkling as his lodge. Far into the night the winter tales stretched and Glooskap's eyelids got heavier and heavier until at last he fell into a deep sleep.

For six months Glooskap slept. During these six long months, his messenger, Loon, had been looking for him. Loon had heard of a warm country far, far to the south, and in this country lived a very powerful woman. Perhaps she was the only one on earth who was more powerful than Winter? Maybe she could persuade him to return to his own country.

Hungry and groggy from his sleep, Glooskap listened carefully. Loon described the route that lead southward and Glooskap decided to go in search of this powerful woman.

Off he went to the seashore. There in the midst of the roaring waves and driving snow, he sang a medicine song to call to his whale friend. Whale quickly answered this call and Glooskap climbed onto his back.

Now, whales have a very strange law that governs those travelling by whale: all such travellers must close their eyes and keep them closed, no matter what; otherwise, the whale could run aground and the traveller could be drowned. Glooskap promised to keep his eyes closed.

Day and night the whale swam on, and each day the seawaters became warmer and warmer, and the air sweeter and sweeter. Finally when they were no longer in deep deep water, the clams, who had seen many a big whale beached in the shallow waters, called out in warning. "Big Sister, Big Sister, go back to the sea. There is danger in these waters for one as big as thee!" Unfortunately for Whale, she did not understand Clam langage, but Glooskap did. (And as we all know, Glooskap himself could be quite a trickster, using things to his own advantage.)

Anxious to be on dry land, when he felt they were close enough to the shore so that he wouldn't have to get wetter than he already was, Glooskap opened *one eye*! The mighty whale came to a sudden stop. Umph, Glooskap was hurled through the air and landed on the sandy shore.

Smiling to himself, he shook more sand from his moose robe, scanned the countryside until he sighted the rainbow trail, then headed for the southland and the mysterious woman.

From a clearing not far ahead, he could hear strains of melody and laughter. Creeping carefully, so as not to startle anyone, Glooskap wove his way through the trees to the clearing. There he stood entranced, watching the most beautiful people he had ever seen. With flowers in their hair and in their hands they danced and sang. So awed was he that he did not notice for some time the old woman standing beside him, watching and smiling as he was.

"Who are those people?"

With her old eyes dancing, the woman answered lovingly, "See the one in the center, she is Summer, the daughter of Dawn and the most beautiful ever born. The others are her children, children of light, sunshine and flowers." The old woman nodded and went on her way as Glooskap sat down to think.

How could he persuade Summer to come north? How?

Singing another of his magical songs, Glooskap began to cut his moose robe into a long slender cord. Lured by the melody, Summer left her circle of companions. Where was this medicine song coming from?

Glooskap was speechless when Summer smiled down on him with questioning eyes. Then fumbling for words and afraid of saying the wrong thing, he seized Summer, held her tightly and started his long journey home. There was no time to mark the trail as he usually would have done, so he unwound the moose robe cord as he ran.

Now Summer's children could not find their mother. They ran through the fields and forests calling her and crying when she did not answer. For weeks they cried. Old Grandmother Dawn tried her best to comfort them, but finally she could offer no more consolation. Gathering the children around her she sighed and covered everything with dark, heavy clouds.

When Glooskap reached his homeland, he could find none of his people! They were all under Winter's spell, sleeping. The whole countryside was cold and quiet. Summer understood then why he had seized her and was so determined to hurry home.

On they trekked to Winter's lodge. The giant, thinking to charm these two into sleep and silence, invited them in. But try as he could and try as he would with his ancient stories and charms, Winter was unable to put Glooskap and the beautiful woman to sleep. Night after night, he spun tales. Night after night his power waned. His frosty charms, blustery spells and crystal lodge began to melt. Summer's strange, smiling presence brought droplets of sweat to his giant brow. Her warmth was discomforting. The deep snow grew heavy and began to melt. Buds appeared on the waking trees. Patches of green pushed aside patches of snow, and Glooskap's people began to yawn and stretch themselves awake.

This woman had unquestionable power! Winter trembled and cold tears trickled down his weathered cheeks.

Summer, being as warm in her heart as in her presence, proposed to Winter that if he returned to the northland she would never disturb or even visit him there, but since he seemed to enjoy Glooskap's country he could remain there for six months and during that time she would return to her own country, for she could not bear to leave her children forever.

Uncomfortably weak in the warmth, Winter could do nothing but gracefully accept Summer's offer. She had proposed an agreement that suited both of them very well. He gathered his belongings and headed north to build a new lodge, and it is there, in the far, far north where he still lives without interference.

When Winter does return for his six month stay, Summer leaves (with her children) for the southland. With the colorful birds following, they paint the leaves as a bright reminder to Winter of the agreement. Then taking hold of the slender moose robe cord, Summer follows the trail home, her children and colorful birds flocking behind.

Reprinted with permission from Ontario Indian, *now* Sweetgrass. *Vol. 5, No. 1.*

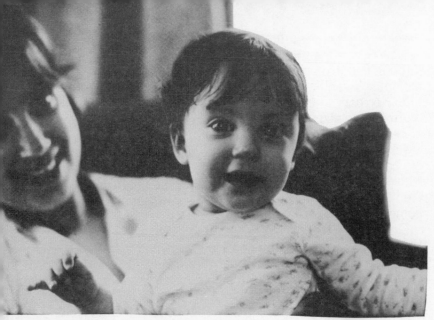

Top and bottom photos, children at the Sagamuk Reserve in Ontario; right, participants at Native American Cultural Day in New York City.

Family Talk

This family speaks of spirit-walk
as we sit around the kitchen
table in the afternoon.
Grey light from the window
corners with woodstove
red. The tea pot boils.

It comes to us sooner or later.
She agreeing goes on at length, how
the tiny bird flew into the home
circled twice and vanished
from a closed room. Must have been
death's hand or at least a forewarning,
They agree.

This is no joking it is Sunday talk
The tea is strong the fire hot. To me
they say do not touch.
I am the youngest
the one who feeds birds, letting them
land on me like whispers.
I feel without a thought of what lies on.
I am all ears.

—Armand Ruffo

Armand Ruffo has lived close to his mother's Ojibway heritage and also to his father's Italian roots. It is from this mixed heritage that his literary voice has developed. "I am a Metis Canadian in the contemporary sense of the term."

"Family Talk" was originally published in The Blue Cloud Quarterly, *Vol. 27, No. 4, Marvin, SD. It is reprinted with permission. Ruffo is also the author of "Protect the Island," page 30.*

TRADITION

The Coming of the Kachinas
by Jerry Kammer

The kachinas entered the village as light began to build in the west, behind a long wall of heavy clouds. The half moon was directly overhead, and in its pale light, smoke was wafting from the metal pipes that reached from the roofs of every home on the plaza. It was the day of the Bean Dance, the day the kachinas returned to the villages.

One pair of kachinas wore white buckskin capes that reached to their ankles. Their masks were also of buckskin, painted with simple designs. Around their necks they wore wreaths of juniper, and on their feet they wore moccasins.

As they approached each of the pueblo houses, the kachinas yelped more loudly, summoning the woman of the house to the door. She sprinkled them with corn meal in a sign of welcome. A young boy of five or six clutched his mother's dress and stared in hushed amazement at these strange creatures, these sacred kachinas who, he already knew, were so important to all people.

A kachina held out a small kachina doll tied to a small bundle of bean sprouts. Timidly the child held out his hand to receive the present. "Asquale," his mother said several times. "Thank you." The kachinas resumed their contented yelping, and the woman answered "Ooh ay, Ooh ay," ("Yes, Yes,") letting them know she shared their happiness and welcomed them to the village of Mishongnovi.

One of the kachinas handed the woman a bundle he had been carrying at his side. She untied it, added several rolls of the parchment-thin, brittle and delicious piki bread, and a single loaf of the round bread Hopi women bake in the beehive ovens outside their homes. With another yelp of appreciation, the kachinas moved on to the next home, where they were greeted by a Hopi mother and a teenage girl wearing the purple and yellow track suit of the Phoenix Indian School.

The new ways are persistent and have a strong appeal for many of the Hopis. And so, television antennas grow like metal cornstalks from the roofs above some homes, where the tube can be plugged into the pickup truck. Some Hopi children may turn from watching the kachinas to watching Saturday morning cartoons.

It is easy to drive past Mishongnovi and never realize it is there. It is perched several hundred feet above the level of the desert floor, atop Second Mesa, about a mile south of Arizona Highway 264. The profile the village presents against the massive blue sky betrays nothing more than the boulder-strewn contours common to the mesa country of northern Arizona. And the pueblo homes, made from the sandstone of the mesa, have a natural protective coloration.

The Bean Dance, or Powamu, occurs in February and marks the kachinas' first procession through the villages. The kachinas are ancestors of the Hopis who, in varied and magnificent forms, carry the prayers of the people. Some kachinas represent animal spirits, others represent plants, others a concept like "sunrise."

What is perhaps most striking to the visitor to Hopiland is the realization that the very young Hopi children—those six or seven and younger who are awaiting initiation—still believe that the kachinas are awesomely powerful creatures who live half the year in the San Francisco Peaks near Flagstaff and the other six months among the Hopis. It is only when they are initiated that they will learn that the kachinas are really people they know personifying the spirits of the universe.

Now the Hopis are protected from crop failures and starvation by salaried jobs, canned food in village stores, and—if necessary—welfare checks. And so the feeling of dependency on natural forces, a feeling that is the creative principle of all religion, has been diluted. Fewer and fewer young Hopi men are willing to accept the discipline and austerity demanded by the Hopi priesthood. There is less adherence to the ancient scheme for common survival.

There is no question that most Hopis welcome the benefits of progress and change. But being a part of America is a profound and difficult challenge to a people whose traditions and life instinct find expression in rituals like the Bean Dance—when the kachinas come to the villages.

This article originally appeared in The Indian Trader, *March, 1980. It is excerpted with permission.*

"At Our Place"

by Eric Anoee

Why is the Inuit tradition different today? If two generations one hundred years apart would meet, their question would be: "Are you an Inuk?" They would even have difficulty recognizing who is the real Inuk.

A modern person would ask: "Where are the rest of your people?"

"At our place," would be the answer.

Two people, one from the past and the other person, a modern type, were talking about their culture. The modern man asked, "Why are you around here, where there is nothing for you?"

"I am where there is food to survive, even if hard times come sometimes. This place is where my father used to live."

Then the Inuk from the past asked: "Where did you come from since I never saw you before?"

"I came from the place I live and flew up here; I travelled in half a day. If I had walked, it would have taken many days. I am confused because I don't know what you use to live upon the land and I don't really believe that you can exist as you say you do. Can you then tell me what is the most important thing in your way of life?"

To this question, the Inuk from the past answered: "As long as our children have something to eat and we are lucky in getting some food, there is nothing we need besides that." This question was asked of the modern Inuk: "What is it that you are tring so hard to live for?"

"I see many fine things in the place where I live, and I want to get as many things as I can."

The Inuk from the past then answered and said: "I don't believe your words because I haven't seen any new things besides the ones I have made."

On facing page, "At Our Place" written in Inukitut, the syllabic language of the Inuit. Eric Anoee is interviewed in Stories of Survival.

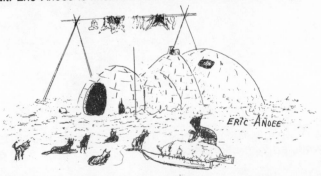

“ᐅᕙᐸᑎᖕᓂ”

ᓱᒐᒥ ᐃᓄᐃᑦ ᐃᓕᕐᑯᓯᖕᒐ ᐊᑦᓚᐅᓕᖅᐸ ᐅᑭᐅᑦ 100 200ᓘᓐᓃᑦ ᑭᖕᒍᕚᕇᒃ ᐊᑯᖕᒐᓂ ᑕᐃᐸᓱᒪᓂᓂᑕᖅ, ᐅᐸᓗᒥᓗ ᐃᓅᔪᖅ ᑲᑎᓇᔭᖅᐸᓂᒃ ᐊᐱᕆᐅᑎᓇᔭᖅᐳᒃ; "ᐃᓅᕖᑦ?" ᓇᓕᐊᑦᓘᓃᑦ ᐃᓄᒻᒪᕆᐅᒐᓗᐊᖅᒪᖕᒌᑦ ᐱᕐᑲᑎᒥᓂᒃ ᐃᓕᑕᖅᓯᓇᔭᖕᒋᓚᖅ. ᓄᑖᒍᓂᕐᓴ ᐊᐱᕆᕗᖅ, "ᓇᐅᒃᓕ ᐃᓚᑎᑦ?" ᐅᕙᐸᑎᓂ. ᐱᕐᑲᑖᓗ ᐃᒃᑐᖕᒐᓂᒃ ᑕᑯᖕᒋᓚᖅ, ᓄᓇᐅᐸ ᐊᐱᓯᒪᔫᐸ ᐊᑦᔨᒋᓯᓐᓇᕐᒪᒍ ᐃᒃᑐᖕᒐ ᑕᐅᑐᒃᑲᓗᐊᕐᒥᐅᒃ ᓱᓇᐅᓱᒋᖕᒋᓛ.

ᑲᑎᓕᓵᖕᒍᐊᕐᑐᒃᓗ ᑕᐃᐸᓱᒪᓂᓂᑕᖅ, ᐅᐸᓗᒥᓂᑕᕐᓗ ᐃᓄᒃ ᐅᕐᑲᓗᕐᑭᖕᒪᓂᒃ ᐃᓅᓯᕆᔭᒥᖕᓂᒃ ᐊᐱᕐᓱᑎᓕᕐᐳᒃ. ᐅᐸᓗᒥᓂᑕᕐᓗ ᐊᐱᕆᕗᖅ, "ᓱᓕᕆᐸᓗᑎᑦᓕ ᑕᒫᓃᐸᐱᑦ ᓱᓇᕐᑲᖕᒋᑐᒥ?" ᐅᕙᖕᒐ ᐃᓅᐸᕕᒋᔪᖕᓇᑕᒫᓂ ᓄᓇᕐᑲᖅᐳᖕᒐ ᓂᕐᑭᒃᓴᕐᓯᐅᕐᓂᓗ ᓄᓇᒥᔭᕐᒪ ᐊᓯᐊᓂ ᐊᔪᕐᓇᕋᔪᖕᒪᑦ, ᑕᒫᓃᐸᖕᒐ ᐊᑖᑕᒪ ᓄᓇᒥᕙᓚᐅᖅᑕᖕᒐᓂ. ᑕᐃᐸᓱᒪᓂᓂᑕᖅ ᐊᐱᕆᓕᖅᐳᖅ, "ᓇᑭᖕᒌᕐᕕᑦᓕ ᑕᑯᓕᒪᓐᓇᖕᒥ ᓚᑎᑦ?" ᓄᓇᒥᔭᒻᒥᓂᑦ ᐊᐅᓚᖅᓯᒪᕗᖕᒐ ᓯᓚᒃᑯᑦ ᕐᑲᒐᑕᐸᓗᖕᒐ, ᐅᐸᓗᐸ ᓇᐸᐸᐃᓇᖕᒐᓂ ᐃᖕᒋᕐᕗᖕᒐ. ᐱᓱᒃᑯᒪᓗ ᐅᐸᓗᓂᒃ ᐊᒥᓱᓂᒃ ᑎᑭᓐᓇᔭᖕᒋᓚᖕᒐ, ᓇᓗᕗᖕᒐᓗ ᐃᓅᓯᕆᔭᐸᓯᖕᓂᒃ ᓱᓇᒥᒃ ᐊᑐᖅᐸᖕᒪᒌᐸᕉ ᐊᑐᓗᐊᖅᑕᓯᓗ ᓱᓇᐅᖕᒪᖕᒌᑖ, ᑕᑯᒐᐸᑭᑦᓕ ᐅᒃᐱᕐᓇᖕᒋᓚᖅ ᐅᕙᐸᑐᑦ ᐃᓅᒐᓗᐊᕐᓂᕈᕕᑦ. ᐅᕐᑲᐅᑎᔪᖕᓇᕐᐱᖕᒐᓕ ᓱᓇ ᐱᔭᕆᐊᕐᑲᕐᓂᕐ ᕚᖕᒍᖕᒪᖕᒌᑦ ᐃᓅᓯᕆᔭᐸᓯᖕᓂ? ᑕᐃᐸᓱᒪᓂᓂᑕᕐᓗ ᑭᐅᕗᖅ, "ᓄᑕᕐᑲᕗᑦ ᓂᕐᑭᒃᓴᕐᑲᑐᐊᖅᐸᑕ, ᐃᔅᓗᒐᐅᒍᐸᑕᐅᓗ ᐊᓯᐊᓂᒃᓕ ᐊᖕᒋᓂᕐᓴᒥᒃ ᐊᒃᓱᕈᑎᕐᑲᖕᒋᓚᖕᒐ." ᐱᕐᑲᑎᓂᓗ ᐊᐱᕆᓕᖅᕚ, "ᐃᒃᕕᓕ ᓱᓇᒥᒃ ᐊᒃᓱᕈᑎᕐᑲᓗᐊᖅᐱᑦ ᐃᓅᑦᔪᑎᒃᓴᓂ? ᐅᐸᓗᒥᓂᑕᕐᓗ ᑭᐅᕗᖅ, "ᐅᕙᖕᒐᓕ ᐱᕐᑯᑎᑦ ᓯᐊᕐᓂᒃ ᐊᒥᓱᓂᒃ ᑕᑯᕙᓕᖅᐳᖕᒐ ᓄᓇᒥᔭᒻᒥ ᐱᕐᑯᑎᑖᕈᒪᕗᖕᒐᓗ ᐊᒥᓱᓂᒃ." ᑕᐃᐸᓱᒪᓂᓂᑕᕐᓗ ᑭᐅᕗᖅ, "ᐅᕐᑲᐅᓯᕆᔭᑎᑦ ᐅᒃᐱᕆᖕᒋᓚᒃᑲ, ᐱᕐᑯᑎᓂᒃ ᐊᒥᓱᓂᒃ ᑕᑯᓚᐅᖅᓯᒪᖕᒋᓇᒪ, ᐱᓕᕆᐊᕐᒃᒪᓗ ᐊᓯᐊᓂᒃ,"

Protect the Island

Across the midsummer sun an aluminum
   boat.
My head begins to knock
like the prop of that motor: suddenly aware
the distance is measured in eyeblinks.

Lifted from a solitude than loons provide
I stand.
Protect the island.
It is a lifesaver.
You can't take it with you.
It is a breath
of fresh air.

Six vacationers land, slurring themselves.
Whiskey walk.
I approach, my inflated lungs full and tense.
They call: where are the fish.
I reply: in the north channel, but the pickerel
are belly-up. The rain is vinegar.

Cursing they say they will write Washington
and Ottawa and it won't be love letters.
They salute, pile into the boat and shove
off. At the shore trees bow in the recent wind
offering the greatest applause.

—Armand Ruffo

Previously published in The Blue Cloud Quarterly, *Vol.
27, No. 4. Marvin, South Dakota. Reprinted with
permission.*

Top, an elder in Eskimo Point, NWT, competes in a game in which a pointed stick is aimed at high speed at the hole carved into a bone suspended from the ceiling; left, an *inukshuk,* a cairn having the rough shape of a human being, used as a landmark in the white Northern landscape; bottom, the Anglican church at Frobisher Bay, NWT is built in the shape of an igloo.

Traditional Legal Ways of the Iroquois Confederacy

By Kaientaronkwen (Ernie Benedict)

Some of the teachings of the Iroquois people say that in the beginning, when there were very few people on earth, there were two ways of looking at society: one authoritative and competitive and the other cooperative. One family would find a good place to live and try to get as much food as possible, fight with others to get more and order people around. Another family would follow the path of cooperation, depend on each other and work together. After many generations, all the Iroquois people, including the family that was competitive, decided together that they would do away with the authority of strength and became cooperative. These rules are still followed and are being revived. And a large part of the Iroquois community still lives by them.

Our community was grouped into clans—groups of families. There were three clans which comprised the General Council: the Bear, the Turtle and the Wolf clans. The Bear clan attached itself to many families from neighboring tribes; most people looked to this clan for leadership. The Turtle clan was the judiciary. The Wolf clan was the keeper of the symbolic well where the questions and issues to be discussed were deposited. The Bear clan carried the executive responsibilities. All the questions were discussed by the Wolf clan and the Bear clan sitting on opposite sides of the fire in front of the Turtle clan. A speaker was appointed to bring the issue under consideration back and forth between the Wolf clan and the Bear clan. When both clans were satisfied with the deliberation it was sent across the fire to the Turtle clan for approval and the law was made. There was a fourth group that sat in the General Council: women. Women listened to the discussions and determined if the discussions were going in accordance with the customs and laws previously established. Women were like the supreme court. They called the messenger if there was any mistake made to bring the matter before the chiefs of those three clans for further discussion.

Cooperative Child-Raising

Now I would like to start again with a new beginning. That is with children and the way they are brought up with this kind of philosophy. Whenever children are disrespectful or when they disobey, often there is an uncle, a grandmother or a grandfather who notices what is happening. The older people have recourse to a store of legends which were handed down from long time ago—and I suspect that many legends were invented on the spot to fit those occasions!—however, many of them have been repeated and they have become *bona fide* legends. These stories carry a moral.

There is one rather complicated story about a rabbit who was proud of what he could do. He had a very fine long tail, very nice, soft and fluffy; he was a very beautiful animal and he liked to call attention to this by running through the forest and by showing off in front of all other animals. One day, he was running in a very strong blizzard and as he ran in a circle he kept beating down the snow, and so after a while the snow piled up under him and he kept building up the pathway. Finally, after a long time, he jumped into the branches of a tree and lay down to sleep. He slept so long that the sun came out and melted the snow, and so there he was at the top of a tall tree. One thing he did not tell all the other animals was that he was a coward. And he was afraid because he was so high. He could not jump or climb down. He did not try. He had no claws. Eventually, he was so hungry that he fell down from the tree and falling, he hit a sharp rock. He split his lip. Coming down through the branches helped to break his fall, but his tail got caught in the tree and today every spring we find a certain tree which is called pussywillow, with fluffs on it which are the remains of the rabbit's tail.

We also teach that the children are part of the community, and they are included in many of the ceremonies. In ceremonies where a diplomat from another tribe comes for a visit he will bring with him greetings, first from the older people. The chiefs also send their greetings, and then mothers and fathers, then there will also be young men and women sending their greetings. All of these are recited separately. The children who are running about in the room and even the babies who are still in the cradle also send their greetings with that delegation—greetings which come in the form of speeches with gifts of wampum or tobacco or a stick with notches carved in it. These are presented as tokens from all the people who have sent their greetings to the host community. Then the answer is also given in similar fashion.

Cooperative Justice

If there is an actual crime that has to be dealt with, a crime that has a great impact on the community, then the council is brought together. The chiefs sit in their appointed space and the council begins. The accused person is brought in and sits in the council with the chiefs. The story then is told and the matter brought back and forth and then the accused person is asked, "As we have told your story to one another, is that the same story that you know?" He will say yes or no, or he or she will make changes. In that way the person pleads his or her own case. Then whether a punishment is needed is discussed. If there is to be a punishment or a judgement, then the person is consulted again: "Do you believe that this is a fitting punishment or recompense for the deed that you have done?" The person accused will think and perhaps discuss it with family or friends (usually the family gathers around) and after everyone has agreed that this is the punishment (often the accused accepts his own punishment), then that is the way the matter is settled.

There is no need of a jailor or policeman to enforce the agreement because the person agreed to what the sentence should be. In this way the system of justice is cooperative rather than coercive.

Our Constitution: Universal Peace

The U. S. Constitution is a constitution which is written. Among the Iroquois, it is recited. Let us look at its preamble! The beginning of the constitution refers to a certain person called a *shaman* who is now called Peacemaker. Many of the Iroquois people refer to this Peacemaker as having established the law of the Iroquois people. One curious thing about this Peacemaker is that he was not from one of original five confederated nations. He was born as a Huron, and Hurons, even at that time, were treated with contempt by the Iroquois people. It was this despised tribe that gave us Tekanawita. These are his words:

"I am the Peacemaker. With the statesmen of the League of Five Nations I plant the Tree of Great Peace. I plant it in your territory, Atotarho and the Onondaga Nation: in the territory of you who are firekeepers. In this territory we plant the Tree of the Great Peace. Under the shade of this Tree of Great Peace, we spread the soft white feathery down of the globe thistle as a seat for you, Atotarho, and your cousin statesmen. There shall you sit and watch the fire of the league of Five Nations. All the affairs of the league shall be transacted at this place before you, Atotarho and your cousin statesmen, by the statesmen of the League of Five Nations.

It is very important document. I think it has had an influence on philosophers of early North American history, and I have read some historians who said that many of these ideals were carried back to Europe and have influenced the politics and political philosophies of authors over there. I left out two things: One is that an eagle will be placed at the top of the tree, for an eagle can see far and give warning of any dangers in the future.

He is also the bird that will fly the highest and he will also relay messages to the Creator above. And so the eagle is very important to the spiritual wellbeing of the people that have gathered below. The other is the fire: The council fire should not be made of chestnut wood. The council fire should be made in such a way that it will not give offense to anyone. So the fire, as a symbol for the thoughts and the words that are spoken there, should be a rather quiet fire that does not have sparks flying in all directions. The wood should not be one that pops and crackles. Chestnut wood pops and crackles and it scatters sparks all over and people could get burned when they sit close to that fire. The council fire must be so carefully built. Now, contrast this council with your own parliament!

STORIES

Hunting

Just about a year ago me and my friend were hunting about ten miles away from where we stayed. Then we went over this big hill. We heard something a close distance away. We didn't know that it was some other hunters. My friend was wearing a brown jacket. Then bang! Just zinged the tree just beside my friend's head. Wow, he was just shaking for fifteen minutes. Then they stop shooting. We layed still. Cracks were coming closer. Then I saw a guy looking at me. He touch me. He said "Thank God, he's alive". We got up, looked at each other. Close call eh? Had a smoke with the Americans. Then they gave my friend a bright orange jacket for his safety. Then it was getting dark, so we headed back to our camping spot. We were followed back. That was those hunters. They camped where we camped. We were close friends from there on. We went home and told some people what happened out here.

Stuart

Survival

Once upon a time I went up in a plane and the plane crashed. I only had an axe, knife, seeds, clothes, matches, traps, and line and hook. It was very cold out. So I lit a match and started a fire. I did not know what to do first. So I took my axe and started to look for good trees. I chopped many trees down and began to build a shelter place. I skinned the tree and made a place. The ground was very cultivated and soft. I looked in my pack sack and there were seeds. I planted them and left. I was very hungry and I took my line and hook. I went to the lake and began to fish. I caught 6 fishes and went back to my shelter place. I made an Indian cooking style. I ate all the fish and went for a walk.

Sarah

Ducks

In Cat Lake there are no cars, but there are lots of skidoos. At night I like to walk around with my buddies. Their names are Isaac and Kevin. They always like to walk around with the girls. My games are shooting pool and baseball in summer. Every summer everybody likes to hunt ducks. Even I like to hunt ducks too. In Cat Lake there are 400 to 500 people. When I hunt ducks I used to go with my brothers and my dad and sometimes I used to go with my buddies too. There are lots of ducks. In summer, maybe more. Lots of ducks this summer. I like to eat ducks in Cat Lake. Everybody likes ducks.

Silas

These stories originally appeared in Everybody Likes Ducks, *stories and poems by the students at the Short Term Emergency Placement Home in Kenora, Ontario, edited by Gregory H. Sparks, 1984. They are reprinted with permission.*

RESOURCES

BOOKS

Adams, Howard. *Prison of Grass: Canada from a Native Point of View.* Toronto: New Press, 1975.

Asch, Michael. *Home and Native Land: Aboriginal Rights and the Constitution.* Toronto and New York: Methuen, 1984.

Axtell James. *The European and the Indian: Essays in the Ethnohistory of Colonial North America.* Toronto and New York: Oxford University Press, 1981.

Barsh, Russo Lawrence and James Youngblood Henderson. *The Road: Indian Tribes and Political Liberty.* Berkeley: University of California Press, 1980.

Berkhoffer, Robert F., Jr. *The White Man's Indian: Images of the American Indian from Columbus to the Present.* New York: Vintage Books, 1978.

Bowden, Henry Warner. *American Indians and Christian Mission.* Chicago: The University of Chicago Press, 1981.

Brand, Johanna. *The Life and Death of Anna Mae Aquash.* Toronto: James Lorimer and Co., 1978.

Brant, Beth. *A Gathering of Spirit: North American Indian Women's Issues.* Amherst: Sinister Wisdom, 1983.

Brown, Joseph Epes. *The Sacred Pipe.* Toronto and New York: Penguin Books, 1971.

_____. *The Spiritual Legacy of the American Indian.* New York: Crossroad Publishing Co., 1982.

Campbell, Maria. *Halfbreed: Biography of a Metis Woman and a Struggle to Gain a Sense of Selfworth.* Toronto: McClelland and Steward.

Campbell, Richard D. *Ganierkeh: People of the Land of Flint.* Lanham: University Press of America, 1985.

Costo, Rupert and Jeanette Henry. *Indian Treaties: Two Centuries of Dishonor.* San Francisco: The Indian Historian Press, 1977.

Culleton, Beatrice. *In Search of April Raintree.* Winnipeg: Pemmican Publications, 1983.

Cumming, Peter and Neil H. Mickenberg. *Native Rights in Canada.* Toronto: General Publishing Co., Ltd., 1972.

DeLoria, Vine, Jr. and Clifford M. Lytle. *American Indians, American Justice.* Austin: University of Texas Press, 1973.

DeLoria, Vine, Jr. *Behind the Trail of Broken Treaties.* New York: Delta Books, 1974.

_____. *Custer Died for Your Sins: An Indian Manifesto.* New York: Avon Books, 1970.

_____. *God Is Red.* New York: Grosset and Dunlop, 1973.

_____. *We Talk, You Listen: New Tribes, New Turf.* New York: Dell, 1974.

Embree, Edwin R. *Indians of the Americas.* New York: Collier Books, 1978.

Farb, Peter. *Man's Rise to Civilization: The Cultural Ascent of the Indians of North America.* New York: Bantam Books, 1978.

Geiogamah, Hanay. *Native American Drama: Three Plays.* Norman: University of Oklahoma Press, 1980.

Getty, Ian A. L. and Antoine Lussier (eds.). *As Long as the Sun Shines and Water Flows: A Reader in Canadian Native Studies.* Vancouver: University of British Columbia Press, 1983.

Highwater, Jamake. *The Sweetgrass Lives On: Fifty Contemporary North American Indian Artists.* New York: Lippincott and Crowell, 1980.

Hirschfelder, Arlene B. *American Indian Stereotypes in the World of Children: A Reader and Bibliography.* Metuchen: The Scarecrow Press, 1982.

Hultkrantz, Ake. *The Study of American Indian Religions.* New York: The Crossroad Publishing Company, 1983.

Jamieson, Kathleen. *Indian Women and the Law in Canada.* Ottawa: Information Canada, 1978.

Johansen, Bruce and Roberto Maestras. *Wasi'chu, the Continuing Indian Wars.* New York: Monthly Review Press, 1979.

Johnston, Emily Paulene. *Legends of Vancouver.* Toronto: McClelland and Stewart, 1961.

Johnston, Patronella. *Tales of Nokomis.* Don Mills: Musson Book Co., 1975.

Josephy, Alvin M. Jr. *Now That the Buffalo's Gone: A Study of Today's American Indian.* New York: Alfred A. Knopf, 1982.

Katz, Jane B. *I am the Fire of Time: The Voices of Native American Women.* E. P. Dutton, 1977.

____. *This Song Remembers: Self-Portrait of Native Americans in the Arts.* Boston; Houghton-Mifflin Co., 1980.

Kenny, George. *Indians Don't Cry.* Toronto: NC Press, Ltd., 1982.

Kleitsch, Christel and Paul Stephens. *A Time to be Brave.* Willowdale: Annick Press, Ltd., 1984.

____. *Dancing Feathers. Ibid.*

Lame Deer, John (Fire) and Richard Erdoes. *Lame Deer: Seeker of Visions:* New York: Washington Square Press.

Lauritzen, Phillip. *Oil and Amulets. Inuit: A People United at the Top of the World.* Anchorage: Breakwater Books, Ltd., 1983.

Little Bear, Leroy, Boldt, Menno, and J. Anthony Long (eds.). *Pathways to Self-Destruction: Canadian Indians and the Canadian State.* Toronto and Buffalo: University of Toronto Press, 1984.

Marquis, Arnold. *Guide to America's Indians: Ceremonials, Reservations and Museums:* Norman: University of Oklahoma Press, 1982.

Mathiessen, Peter. *In the Spirit of Crazy Horse.* New York: Viking Press, 1980.

McCullum, Hugh and Karmel and John Olthuis. *Moratorium: Justice, Energy, the North, and the Native People.* Toronto: Anglican Book Centre, 1977.

McCullum, Hugh and Karmel. *This Land Is Not for Sale. Ibid.,* 1975.

Metayer, Maurice (ed. and translator). *Tales from the Igloo.* New York: St. Martin's Press, 1972.

Momaday, N. Scott. *House Made of Dawn.* New York: Harper and Row, 1966.

Morey, Sylvester M. and Olivia Gillam. *Respect For: The Traditional Upbringing of American Indian Children.* New York: Myrin Institute Books, 1974.

Morris, Alexander. *1880: The Treaties of Canada with the Indians.* Toronto: Coles Publishing Co., 1880, reprinted 1929.

Nabokov, Peter (ed.). *Native American Testimony: An Anthology of Indian and White Relations.* New York: Harper and Row, 1978.

Neihardt, John G. *Black Elk Speaks.* New York: Pocket Books, 1932.

New Mexico People and Energy Collective. *Red Ribbons for Emma.* Stanford: New Seed Press, 1981.

Niethammer, Carol. *Daughters of the Earth: The Lives and Legends of American Indian Women.* New York: MacMillan, 1977.

Ortiz, Simon J. *The People Shall Continue: Fifth World Tales.* San Francisco: Children's Book Press, 1977.

Petrone, Penny. *First People, First Voices.* Toronto and Buffalo: University of Toronto Press, 1983.

Pevar, Stephen L. *The Rights of Indians and Tribes*. New York: Bantam Books.

Pitseolak. *Pitseolak: Pictures Out of My Life*. Toronto: Oxford University Press, 1971.

Schwartz, Herbert T. *Tales from the Smokehouse*. Edmonton: Hurtig Publishers, 1974.

Sealey, D. Bruce and Antoine Lussier. *The Metis: Canada's Forgotten People*. Winnipeg: Pemmican Publications, 1983.

Storm, Hyemeyohsts. *Seven Arrows*. New York: Ballantine Books, 1972.

Talbot, Steve. *Roots of Oppression: The American Indian Question*. New York: International Publishers, 1981.

Tedlock, Dennis and Barbara Tedlock. *Teachings from the American Earth: Indian Religion and Philosophy*. New York: Liveright Publishing Corp., 1975.

Thompson, Stith (ed.). *Tales of the North American Indians*. Bloomington: Indiana University Press, 1966.

Tooker, Elisabeth (ed.). *Native North American Spirituality of the Eastern Woodlands*. New York and Toronto: Paulist Press, 1979.

VanEvery, Dale. *Disinherited: The Lost Birthright of the American Indian*. New York: Avon/Discus, 1980.

VanKirk, Sylvia. *Many Tender Ties: Women in the Fur Trade Society in Western Canada, 1670-1870*. Norman: University of Oklahoma Press, 1983.

Waters, Frank. *The Man Who Killed the Deer*. New York: Washington Square Press, 1970.

Witt, Shirley Hill and Stan Steiner (eds.). *The Way: An Anthology of American Indian Literature*. New York: Random House, 1972.

_____. *Unlearning "Indian" Stereotypes*. New York: Council on Interracial Books for Children.

FILMS

"Along Sandy Trails." 5 minutes, color filmstrip with audio cassette. Available from Viking Press, 625 Madison Avenue, New York, NY 10022.

"Annie and the Old One." 15 minutes, color, 16 mm. Available from ECUFILM, 810 Twelfth Avenue South, Nashville, TN 37202. Rental: $20. 1976

"Another Face of Jesus." 20 minutes, color, filmstrip with audio cassette. Purchase from American Baptist Churches, Valley Forge, PA 19481. $7.50. Revised 1980.

"Arrow to the Sun." 9 minutes, color, filmstrip with audio cassette. Available from Weston Woods, Weston, CT 06883.

"Broken Treaty at Battle Mountain," 60 minutes, color, 16 mm. Available from ECUFILM, 810 Twelfth Avenue South, Nashville, TN 37202. Rental: $12 and from Cinema Guild, 1697 Broadway, Suite 802, New York, NY 10019. Rental $100. 1974.

"Civilized Tribes." 20 minutes, color, 16 mm and video. Available from Cinema Guild, 1697 Broadway, Suite 802, New York, NY 10019. Rental: $50.

"Corn is Life." 19 minutes, color, 16 mm. and video. Available from University of California, Extension Media Center, 2223 Fulton Street, Berkeley, CA 94720. Rental: $33. 1983.

"Crow Dog." 57 minutes, color, 16 mm. Available from Cinema Guild, 1697 Broadway, Suite 802, New York, NY 10019. Rental: $90. 1970.

"Dancing Feathers." 28 minutes, color, 16 mm. and ½" and ¾" video.

Available from Magic Lantern Films, 872 Winston Churchill Boulevard, Oakville, Ontario L6J 4Z2, Canada. Rental:, $59.50. 1984.

"Expressions of Eskimo Culture: Inuit Printmaking and Carving." 30 minutes, color, 16 mm. Available from Michigan Media, The University of Michigan Resources Center, 416 Fourth Street, Ann Arbor, MI 48109. Rental: $20. Purchase: $175. 1980.

"The Four Corners: A National Sacrifice Area?" 58 minutes, color, 16 mm. Available from Bullfrog Films, Oley, PA 19547. Rental: $85. 1983.

"The Good Mind." 30 minutes, color, 16 mm. and video. Available from ECUFILM, 810 Twelfth Avenue South, Nashville, TN 37202. Rental: $15. Purchase: $30. 1983.

"The Great Spirit within the Hole." Color, 16 mm. and ½" and ¾" video. Available from Twin Cities Public Television, 1640 Como Avenue. St. Paul, MN 55108. Film Rental: $55 + $7 handling fee. Video Rental: $35 + $7 handling fee. 1983.

"Haa Shagoon." 29 minutes, color, 16 mm. Available from University of California Extension Media Center, 2223 Fulton Street, Berkeley, CA 94720. Rental: $38. 1983.

"Haudenosaunee: Way of the Longhouse." 13 minutes, color, 16 mm. Available from ECUFILM, 810 Twelfth Avenue South, Nashville, TN 37203. Rental $25 and from Icarus Films, 200 Park Avenue South, Suite 1319, New York, NY 10003. Rental: $35. 1982.

"Homeland." 21 minutes, color, 16 mm. Available from ECUFILM, 810 Twelfth Avenue South, Nashville, TN 37203. Rental: $20.

"I Hear the Owl Call My Name." 78 minutes, color, 16 mm. Available from Learning Corporation of America, 1350 Avenue of the Americas, New York, NY 10019. Rental: $110. 1973.

"An Indian Jesus." 42 frame color filmstrip with reading script and guide. Available from Friendship Press Distribution Center, 7820 Reading Road, Cincinnati, OH 45237. Purchase: $9.50. 1984.

"Last Chance for the Navajo." 28 minutes, color, 16 mm. Available from ECUFILM, 810 Twelfth Avenue South, Nashville, TN 37203. 1977.

"Let My People Live: Native American Health Care." 55 minutes, color, 16 mm or all video formats. Available from Time Life Video Distribution Center, 100 Eisenhower Drive, P.O. Box 644, Paramus, New Jersey 07653. Rental: $85 + 5% handling fee.

"More Than Bows and Arrows." 56 minutes, color, 16 mm. Available from Michigan Media, The University of Michigan Media Resource Center, 416 Fourth Street, Ann Arbor, MI 48109. Rental: $30.30. 1978.

"My Hands are the Tools of My Soul: Art and Poetry of the American Indian." 54 minutes, color, 16 mm. Available from Michigan Media, The University of Michigan Media Resources Center, 416 Fourth Street, Ann Arbor, MI 48109. Rental: $27.95. 1975.

"North American Indians, Part II: How the West was Won and Honor Lost." 60 minutes, color, 16 mm. Available from ECUFILM, 810 Twelfth Avenue South, Nashville, TN 37203. Rental: $12 or from Cinema Guild, 1697 Broadway, Suite 802, New York, NY 10019. Rental $100. 1971.

"The Owl and the Raven." 8 minutes, color, 16 mm. Available from Michigan Media, The University of Michigan Media Resources Center, 415 Fourth Street, Ann Arbor, MI 48109. Rental $10.95. 1974.

"Paul Kane Goes West." 15 minutes, color, 16 mm. Available from Michigan Media Center, The University of Michigan Media Resources Center, 416 Fourth Street, Ann Arbor, MI 48109. Rental: $13.58. 1974.

"People of the Dawn." 30 minutes, color, ½" and ¾" video. Available from ECUFILM, 810 Twelfth Avenue South, Nashville, TN 37203. Rental: $15. 1981.

"The Six Nations." 26 minutes, color, 16 mm and video. Available from the Cinema Guild, 1697 Broadway, Suite 802, New York, NY 10019. Rental: $50.

"Sometimes We Burn, Sometimes We Tremble: an AV Meditation on Native Canadian Spirituality." 22 minutes, color filmstrip, script and cassette tape. Available from the Anglican Church of Canada. Purchase: $15.

"A Song for Dead Warriors." 25 minutes, color, 16 mm. Available from New Time Film Library, P.O. Box 502, New York, NY 10014. Rental: $50. 1973.

"Spirit Bay." ½" and ¾" video. Available from Beacon Films, P.O. Box 575, Norwood, MA 02062. 1984.

"The Sun Dagger." 29 minutes, color, 16 mm. Available from Bullfrog Films, Oley, PA 19547. Rental: $50. (A 58 minute version is available for an $85 rental fee.) 1983.

"A Time to Be Brave." 28 minutes, color, 16 mm. Available from Magic Lantern Films, 872 Winston Churchill Boulevard, Oakville, Ontario L6J 4Z2, Canada. Rental: $59.50 (three days). 1983.

"Unlearning Indian Stereotypes." 15 minutes, color filmstrip with audio cassette. Available from the Council on Interracial Books for Children, 1841 Broadway, New York, NY 10023 or from the American Friends Service Committee, 2161 Massachusetts Avenue, Cambridge, MA 02140. Rental: $20. 1978.

"We Need Help! Lubicon Lake Cree Indians." 18 minutes, color filmstrip with script and audio cassette. Available from SYNESTHETICS, Inc., Box 254, Cos Cob, CT 06807.

"The Yerxas." 26½ minutes, color, 16 mm. Available from Gary Nichol, 424 McLeod Street, Ottawa, Ontario K1R 5P5, Canada.

ORGANIZATIONS

American Friends Service Committee. 1501 Cherry Street, Philadelphia, PA 19102.

Americans for Indian Opportunity. 1010 Massachusetts Avenue, NW, Suite 200, Washington, DC. 20006. Newsletter.

Arrow, Inc. 1000 Connecticut Avenue, NW, Suite 501, Washington, DC 20036.

Assembly of First Nations. 222 Queen Street, 5th floor, Ottawa, Ontario K1P KV9, Canada.

Association on American Indian Affairs, Inc. 432 Park Avenue South, New York, NY 10016.

Association for Native Development in the Visual and Performing Arts. 27 Carlton Street, Suite 208, Ottawa, Ontario K2P OG3, Canada.

Bureau of Indian Affairs, Public Information Office. 18th Street and E Street, NW, Washington, DC 20245.

Canadian Alliance in Solidarity with Native Peoples (CASNP). 16 Spadina Road, Toronto, Ontario M5R 2S7, Canada. Newsletter.

Department of Indian Affairs and Northern Development. Les Terrasses de la Chaudiere, Ottawa, Ontario K1A OH4, Canada.

Indian Rights Association. 1505 Race Street, Philadelphia, PA 19102. Magazine.

Indian Rights for Indian Women. 19 Sackville Street, Toronto, Ontario M5A 3E1, Canada.

Institute for Development of Indian Law. 927 15th Street, NW, Washington, D.C. 2000. Newsletter, publications.

International Indian Treaty Council, 777 UN Plaza, Room 10F, New York, NY 10017.

Inuit Tapirisat Canada. 176 Gloucester Street, Ottawa, Ontario, Canada.

National Association of Friendship Centres, 200 Cooper Street, Suite 3, Ottawa, Ontario K2P OG1, Canada.

National Tribal Chairman's Association. 1701 Pennsylvania Avenue, NW, Suite 406, Washington, DC 20006.

National Coalition to Support Indian Treaties. 710 North 43rd Street, Seattle, WA 98103.

National Congress of American Indians, 202 E Street, NE, Washington, DC 20002.

National Indian Youth Council, Inc. 201 Hermosa, NE, Albuquerque, NM 87108.

Native Council of Canada. 170 Laurier Avenue West, 5th floor, Ottawa, Ontario K1P 5V5, Canada.

Native Women's Association of Canada. 222 Queen Street, 5th floor, Ottawa, Ontario L1R 5V9 Canada.

New Mexicans for Tribal Development. 525 San Pedro, NE, Suite 106, Albuquerque, NM 87108.

North American Indian Museum Association. 466 Third Street, Niagara Falls, NY 14301.

Project North. 80 Sackville Street, Toronto, Ontario M5A 3E5, Canada. Newsletter.

United States Commission on Civil Rights. 1121 Vermont Avenue, NW, Washington, DC 20425.

OTHER RESOURCES

CATALOGUES

Akwesasne Notes Catalogue. Akwesasne Notes, Mohawk Nation, Roose-veltown, NY 13683.

Books about Indians. Museum of the American Indian, Broadway and 155th Street, New York, NY 10032.

Canadian Indian Policy: A Critical Bibliography by Robert J. Surtees. Published for the Newberry Library by Indiana University Press, 10th and Morton Sts., Bloomington, IN 47401.

Directory of North American Indian Museusm and Cultural Centers. North American Indian Museum Association, 466 Third Street, Niagara Falls, NY 14301.

Film and Video Catalogue. The Cinema Guild, 1697 Broadway, Suite 802, New York, Y 10019

Minneapolis Public Schools: An Annotated Bibliography of the Indian Elementary Curriculum. Minneapolis Public Schools, Planning, Development, Evaluation Department, Northeast Broadway, Minneapolis, MN 55413.

National Film Board of Canada. 1 Lombard Street, Toronto, Ontario M5C 1J6, Canada. (In the U.S., write to: National Film Board of Canada, 1251 Avenue of the Americas, 16th Floor, New York, NY 10020.)

Native Americans on Film and Video, edited by Elizabeth Weatherford. Museum of the American Indian, Broadway and 155th Street, New York, NY 10032.

Native Resource Directory. National Native American Cooperative, P.O. Box 5000, San Carlos, AZ 85550-0301.

On Film. Department of Indian Affairs, Audio Visual Services, Les Terrasses de la Chaudiere, Ottawa, Ontario K1A OH4, Canada.

MAPS

Indian Land Areas. Bureau of Indian Affairs, 18th Street and E Street, NW, Washington, DC 20245.

Indian Linguistic and Cultural Affiliations. Department of Indian Affairs, Les Terrasses de la Chaudiere, Ottawa, Ontario K1A OH4, Canada.

"Indians of North America," December 1972 and "Alaska," January 1984. *National Geographic Magazine,* 17th and M Streets, NW, Washington, DC 20036.

Map'n'Facts: Native Peoples of North America. Friendship Press, 1985. $4.50.

POSTERS

Akwesasne Notes, Mohawk Nation, Rooseveltown, New York 13683.

Publications Division, Department of Information, Government of the Northwest Territories, Yellowknife, Northwest Territories X1A 2L9, Canada.

PUBLICATIONS

Akwesasne Notes. Mohawk Nation, Rooseveltown, NY 13683.

Alive Now. Sept./Oct. 1984. (Vol. 14, No. 5). The Upper Room, 1908 Grand Avenue, P.O. Box 189, Nashville, TN 37202.

Sweetgrass. 90 Nolan Court, Unit 46, Markham, Ontario L3R 9Z9, Canada.

Turtle Quarterly. The Native American Center for the Living Arts, Inc., 25 Rainbow Mall, Niagara Falls, NY 14303.

Washington Newsletter. Friends Committee on National Legislation, 245 Second Street, NE, Washington, DC 20002.

(The U.S. Bureau of Indian Affairs and the Canadian Department of Indian Affairs have listings of regional publications. See listings under Organizations.)

PUBLISHERS

The Indian Historian Press. 1451 Masonic Avenue, San Francisco, CA 94117.

Pemmican Publications. 701-310 Broadway Avenue, Winnipeg, Manitoba R3C OS6, Canada.

RECORDINGS

Boot Records, Ltd. 1343 Matheson Boulevard East, Mississauga, Ontario L4W 1R1, Canada. (Catalogue of Inuit and Indian recordings available).

Caedmon Records, Inc. 1995 Broadway, New York, NY 10023. (Records and cassettes of legends.)

Ethnic Folkways Records. 17 West 60th Street, New York, NY. (Catalogue available.)

Native Development in the Visual and Performing Arts. (See listing under Organizations.)

MUSEUMS WITH FOCUS ON NATIVE PEOPLES

Alaska Indian Arts
Port Chilkoot
Haines, AK 99827

American Museum of
  Natural History
79th Street and Central Park West
New York, NY 10024

Cherokee National
  History Museum
Post Office Box 515
Tahlequah, OK 74464

Chickasaw Council
  House Museum
Route 1, Box 14
Tishomingo, OK 73460

Five Civilized Tribes Museum
Honor Heights Drive
Muskoge, OK 74401

Institute of American Indian
  Arts Museum
Cerillos Road
Santa Fe, NM 87501

Mohave Museum of History
  and Arts
400 West Beale
Kingman, AZ 86401

Museum of Albuquerque
Yale Boulevard, 5E
Post Office Box 1293
Albuquerque, NM 87103

Museum of the American Indian
Broadway at 155th Street
New York, NY 10032

Museum of Anthropology
6393 NW Marine Drive
Vancouver V6T 1W5
British Columbia, Canada

Museum of Navajo Ceremonial Art
704 Camion Lejo
Post Office Box 5153
Santa Fe, MN 87501

Museum of the Plains Indians
  and Craft Center
Post Office Box 400
Browning, MT 59417

National Museum of History
  and Technology
Smithsonian Institution
14th Street and Constitution Avenue
Washington, DC 20560

Navajo Tribal Museum
Post Box 797
Window Rock, AZ 86515

Royal Ontario Museum
100 Queen's Park
Toronto M5S 2C6
Ontario, Canada

Thomas Gilcrease Institute of
  American History and Art
2500 W. Newton, Route 6
Tulsa, OK 74127

Ute Indian Museum
735 N. Third
Montrose, CA 81401

Woolaroc Museum
Route 3
Bartlesville, OK 74003